The MIGHTY BIG BOOK OF TRAVEL MYSTERIES

D0040581

The Mighty Big Book of Travel Mysteries

GALLERY O' GAMES

Portions previously published in *The Case of the Missing Lynx*, *A Dog Gone Dilemma*, *Trapped in Hill House*, *Detective Dave's Bummer Vacation*, and *The Invisible Suitcase*.

Library of Congress Cataloging-in-Publication Data is available.

ISBN 0-8431-7734-9   A B C D E F G H I J

PSS! and Mighty Big Books are registered trademarks of
Penguin Putnam Books for Young Readers.

The MIGHTY BIG BOOK OF TRAVEL MYSTERIES

GALLERY O' GAMES

PSS!
PRICE STERN SLOAN

The Invisible Suit Case

1 wrote Dr. Carson's address in my notebook, but I can't seem to find it. Perhaps you could circle it for me.

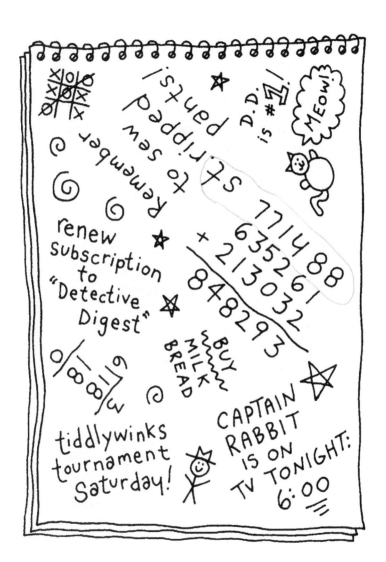

You're more than welcome to join me. I'm sure you won't get in the way. We'll have to take the subway since my car is at the mechanic's. Hmmm, if we want to get to Consternation Station, do we take the A, B, or C train?

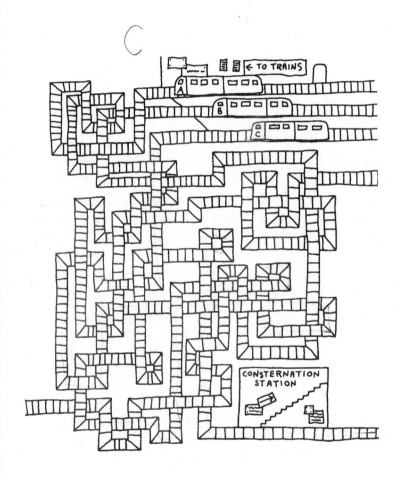

13

Dr. Carson said she would meet us here. She told me she'd either be wearing a flowered skirt and a striped blouse, *or* a striped skirt and a polka dot blouse. I don't see her anywhere, do you?

Pleased to meet you, Detective Dave, and your friend as well," said Dr. Carson.

"I have a very important matter to discuss with you, but I'd rather not arouse suspicions by having us seen together. You two take the elevator to my office on the fifth floor where we can talk privately. I'll meet you there."

Gee, I wish Dr. Carson would have explained how to use this elevator before she disappeared. If we want to get to the fifth floor, which buttons should we push?

3 floor: CBADGHIL.ONM

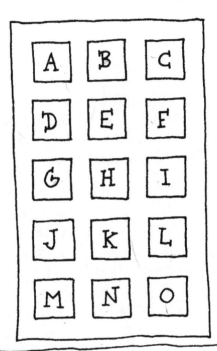

We're on the correct floor, but which office is Dr. Carson's? If she wants our talk to be private, we'd better not knock on the wrong door. Which door should we try?

ome in. I'm glad the two of you didn't have any trouble finding my office. The reason I need your help, Detective Dave, is because this afternoon at the Science Museum I will be unveiling my latest invention. I'd like you there in case someone tries to steal it. Here's a description of my invention. The description is in code, but I'm sure a great mind like yours won't have any trouble reading it."

This is hard! Hey! Let's try a trick I learned when I was working as an undercover agent for the president. Try starting from the center and read outward.

```
T S E T A E R G Y M T B U O
I L P M O C T I U S E H T D
N E T I U S A S I N O I S A
V T O E K A M O T Y A T R T
E E F S F E V A H I W N A U
N L I O I D F O S K A E E O
T Y N M N I T F R R D V W H
I D V E A F E A A O E N R T
O I I O L F R Y E W R I E I
N S S N L I C U L T E Y V W
E A I E Y D I S C O V M E S
V P B I N V I S I B L E O I
E P L E C L O T H E S W H T
R E A R S F R O M V I E W I
```

r. Carson gave me this map and said we should meet her at the Science Museum as soon as possible. That's odd...none of the buildings are labeled, and I wonder what the code at the bottom of the map means.

This is starting to look very familiar. I think we passed that building, don't you?

Which building do *you* think is the Science Museum?

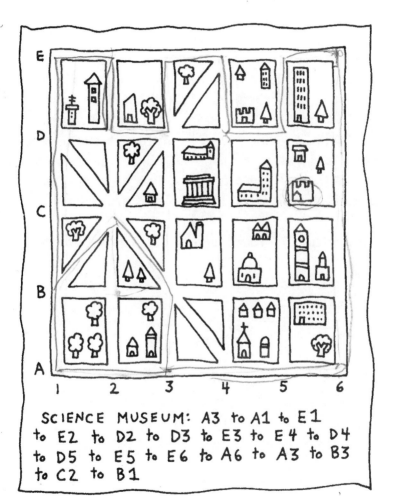

SCIENCE MUSEUM: A3 to A1 to E1 to E2 to D2 to D3 to E3 to E4 to D4 to D5 to E5 to E6 to A6 to A3 to B3 to C2 to B1

23

It's a good thing you figured out that map! Getting to the museum was easy. Dr. Carson will be giving her presentation in one of these rooms. But I've forgotten which one. I do, however, remember that there are three words in the room's name and each word has a different number of letters.

You locate the room while I get a drink of water.

MUSEUM DIRECTORY

UPSTAIRS
ASTRONOMICAL DISCOVERIES OBSERVATORY
EXPLORATION ROOM
CHATTERBOX LECTURES AUDITORIUM

EAST WING
MARIE CURIE STUDY
BUNSEN BURNER LAB
WASHINGTON CARVER MEMORIAL HALL
SCIENTIFIC BREAKTHROUGHS AUDITORIUM

WEST WING
BIG IDEA ROOM
NOAH GUDEAL HALL
FOSSILS AND BONES EXHIBIT
GREAT INVENTORS AUDITORIUM

BASEMENT
AMAZING WONDERS ROOM
EINSTEIN THEATER
ANCIENT CULTURES EXHIBIT

Here's the right room and there's Dr. Carson, but I wonder why she looks so upset. "Quick! Someone just grabbed the box containing my invisible suit! He ran down the hallway and out one of these doors."

We'd better hurry! Pick the door the thief used. I'll be right behind you.

ats! Dr. Carson's box is empty. The thief must be wearing the invisible suit! Rats! This vacant lot is filled with rats! Lead us out of this lot without passing any rats—they make me nervous.

t sounds like something is wrong next door at the pet shop. Maybe that's where the thief went. "Somebody help me! I was alone in my store when the lid to the snake box floated off by itself. Then someone grabbed my glasses and now I can't see anything!"

It must have been the thief in the invisible suit! Help the pet shop owner find her glasses and the five escaped snakes. I think I hear footsteps running down the sidewalk.

FISH FOOD

SNAKES

DOG FOOD

NEWTS

ook! Not only has the thief mixed up the titles on this sidewalk gallery, but he's also turned the pictures sideways and upside down. You help the artist match the titles to the pictures and decide which way the paintings should hang. I think I hear the thief laughing up ahead.

MY PET GOOSE

PICTURES by PAT

SELF-PORTRAIT

ROCKY MOUNTAIN LANDSCAPE

KING KONG

EGYPTIAN MORNING

The thief passed this way, too. He's stolen 8 things from this cafe scene. You draw in the missing objects; I'm going to see if I can catch up with that crook!

Foo-ey! I heard the crook run into the park, but this guard won't let us in without tickets.

"Tickets cost one cent for every brick in this gate, and if you don't pay the *exact* amount, I won't let you in."

I'll pay for the tickets if you count carefully and tell me how much it will cost for the two of us.

PARK ENTRANCE

Oh no, the thief has struck again! He's changed two letters on each of these signs. You correct the signs while I figure out where he might have gone next.

38

I'm getting hungry. Perhaps the thief is too, and will try his hand at stealing lunches. I think we should check out the picnic areas. *Without crossing or retracing your path,* visit each of the shelters in order and report back to me.

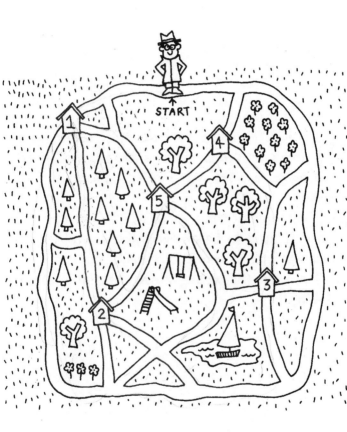

START

No luck? I didn't find the thief either, but I think he dropped this shoe. If this kid will let us use his dog, maybe he can sniff out the crook.

"Sure, you can borrow my dog...if you can guess his name. It used to be on his collar—until all the dog tags fell off. Watch out, though. If you call him by the wrong name, he won't be very happy."

43

That dog took off like a bullet when he sniffed this shoe, and now he's barking up that tree. I think we found the thief! Throw down that suit of clothes, you crook! Hurry, shade in all the spaces that have a dot to see what appears!

1 'm taking this thief down to the police station. You call Dr. Carson and tell her we have recovered her invisible suit. I'm not sure of her *exact* phone number, but here are enough clues for you to figure it out.

A. EITHER THE FIRST THREE DIGITS ARE THE SAME OR THE LAST THREE DIGITS ARE THE SAME.

B. THE FOURTH DIGIT IS MORE THAN 7.

C. THERE ARE NO 8s IN THE NUMBER.

D. THE SECOND DIGIT IS FOUR LESS THAN THE FOURTH DIGIT.

E. THE SIXTH DIGIT IS 2.

F. THE SUM OF THE FIFTH AND SIXTH DIGIT EQUALS THE SEVENTH DIGIT.

G. THERE IS A 6 SOMEPLACE IN THE NUMBER.

$$\underline{\quad}\ \underline{\quad}\ \underline{\quad}\ -\ \underline{\quad}\ \underline{\quad}\ \underline{\quad}\ \underline{\quad}$$
  1   2   3   4   5   6   7

The thief typed this confession at the police station. Unfortunately he used a broken typewriter and all the vowels (A, E, I, O, U) came out wrong. I sure would like to know who the thief was and his motive for stealing the suit. If you replace the mixed-up vowels with the correct ones, we'll both know.

YOS, A STULO DR. CERSUN'S
ANVASABLO SIAT. A EM E
SCHUUL PRANCAPEL END A EM
ELWEYS THO UNO WHU HES TU
PINASH STIDONTS WHU
MASBOHEVO. A THUIGHT THET
AF A WES ANVASABLO, AT
WUILD GAVO MO THO CHENCO
TU MASBOHEVO FUR UNCO.

The punishment they gave the thief was a little severe, but maybe he deserved it. I think you are clever enough to crack this code and find out what the police are making the thief do!

AYCH-EE

AYCH-AY-ESS

TEA-OH

SEA-EL-EE-AY-EN

TEA-AYCH-EE

ESS-SEA-AYCH-OH-OH-EL

EL-YOU-EN-SEA-AYCH-ARE-OH-OH-EM

EF-OH-ARE

OH-EN-EE

DOUBLEYOU-AYCH-OH-EL-EE

WHY-EE-AY-ARE !

Another case solved by the one and only Detective Dave! Dr. Carson rewarded me with a lifetime supply of invisible ink—perfect for writing letters to other stupendous sleuths.

You haven't been forgotten either. To discover my reward to you, connect these dots in the order indicated at the bottom of the page.

4-5-6-5-18
11-7-8-9-14
57-56-59-58
43-42-46-63
53-36-55-54-52
24-37-30-24
44-45
31-33-32-47

14-26-27-29-28-39
62-60-41-60-40-61
23-13-26-25-12-21-23
11-21-19-20-22-38-39
17-3-2-1-16
35-51-50-48-34-49
10-15

The Case of the Missing Lynx

That was the mail carrier with this letter marked "URGENT." I hope it's not another overdue rent notice from my landlord. I had better open it and see what it says.

Hmmm...doesn't make much sense. I've got an idea. Here's a trick I learned while working as an undercover agent for the president. Cross out every five-letter word in the note and see if that helps.

DETECTIVE DAVE -

SMILE IF YOU ENJOY MUSIC

THOSE GOATS ARE CLEVER ENOUGH TO WRITE BOOKS

DECODE THIS CRAZY NOTE,

THEN PERHAPS YOU WILL LAUGH

YOU'LL NEVER BE ABLE TO HELP ME.

PLEASE COME AT NIGHT

ONCE AGAIN THREE DUCKS TRIED TO CRUSH THE CITY

ZOO. GOERS FOUND SOMETHING TERRIBLE

LUNCH HAS HAPPENED TWICE TODAY.

T. J.

Great work! Hop in the car and we're off to the zoo. I'm not good with maps, so I'll let you find the way for us. Watch out for all the one-way streets; we can only pass over an arrow if we are heading in the same direction that the arrow points. Remember: if there is no arrow then we can go in either direction.

We need to find T.J.'s office, but this zoo directory doesn't seem to be of much help; all of the first and last names have fallen off. If you put the names back in their proper places, one letter per blank, we'll know who has the initials T.J.

Zoo Director _ _ _   _ _ _ _ _ _ _ _ _
room 101

Feeding Supervisor _ _ _ _ _ _   _ _ _ _ _
room 102

Secretary _ _ _ _ _   _ _ _ _ _ _ _ _
room 103

Head of Security _ _ _ _   _ _ _ _ _ _ _
room 104

Gardener _ _ _ _ _ _ _ _   _ _ _ _ _ _ _
room 105

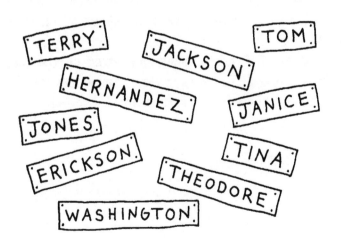

This looks like the right office, and that woman waving us in must be T.J.

"Detective Dave! I'm so thankful you came. And I see that you've brought an assistant. Please come in, both of you. Something dreadful has happened, and the zoo desperately needs your help. It's so awful I can't even talk about it. I'll have to write it down for you."

Oh dear! T.J. is so upset she mixed up the letters in every word. You unscramble the words to find out the problem; I'll try to calm T.J. down.

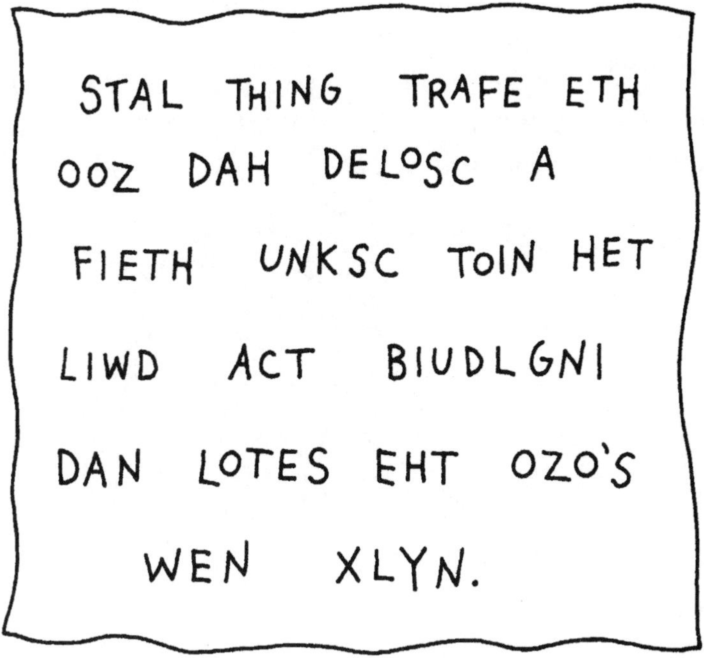

STAL THING TRAFE ETH

OOZ DAH DELOSC A

FIETH UNKSC TOIN HET

LIWD ACT BIUDLGNI

DAN LOTES EHT OZO'S

WEN XLYN.

Let's go question the guards who were on duty last night.

I suspect that only one guard is lying, but I don't know who. If only *one* guard is *not* telling the truth, which guard is it?

ood going! When confronted, the guilty guard admitted to having fallen asleep on duty. That must have been when the lynx was stolen.

Our next step is to investigate the scene of the crime. T. J. has given me a set of keys, but I can't remember which key is for the lynx cage. If we try the wrong key, it will set off the alarm system. I do remember that key #1, labeled "A," is for the BEAR cage. Using that information, can you figure out which key we need?

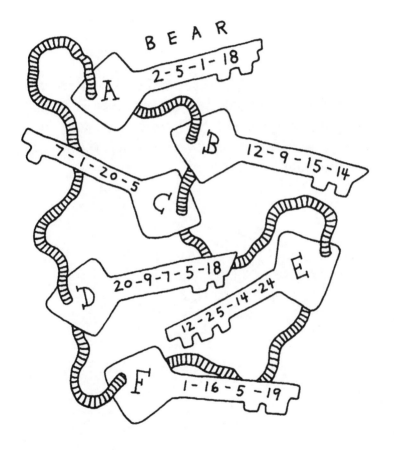

BEAR
A 2-5-1-18

B 12-9-15-14

7-1-20-5 C

D 20-9-7-5-18

E
12-25-14-24

F 1-16-5-19

69

It looks like the inside of the cage is empty. Oh, I see you've found something. It looks like a map. The thief must have gone to Jake's, but I can't tell which building that would be, can you?

This must be the right place, but which apartment is Jake's? Let's ask this man leaving the building.

"Jake? Yeah, he lives here. In fact, he lives on the same floor as I do. But not next door to me. Just today Mrs. Wu was saying that she's glad she doesn't live next door to Jake either because he's so loud. Mrs. Wu and I live directly on either side of Mr. Wagner, the quietest person on the floor. I live in apartment #1 and Jake lives in apartment... sorry, that's my taxi. I gotta go!"

All this thinking has given me a headache. You figure out where Jake lives and I'll go take an aspirin.

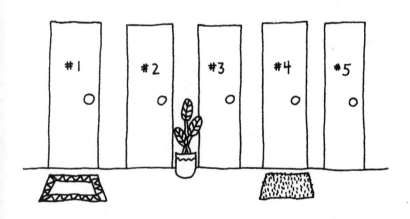

Now that we know which apartment is his, let's see if Jake's home. Ooops! There he goes out the back door, and he triple-locked the door. Quick, search the room! If we find the three keys to the door, maybe we can still catch him.

We're too late.
But look at this: Jake must have dropped
these pieces of paper when he ran out.
Jigsaw puzzles were always hard for me, but I bet
that by studying which sides of the pieces are torn,
you can rewrite the note in the grid below.

This café seems really small. I don't see anyplace here where someone could hide. I don't know about you, but I'm getting hungry. I wonder what they're serving for lunch today. Say, look at the soup menu. There's something weird about it. I have a hunch that it's a clue as to where Jake's hiding, but I can't figure it out. Can you?

TRy A cuP of
DeliciOus sOup

cReam of mUshroom
corN chowDER
cream of aspaRagUs
veGetable

Good job! This must be the way to the secret hideout. You lead the way down these dirt tunnels, I'll be right behind you.

PRIVATE

ha! We've found Jake! And I recognize him as a crook with a long history of selling stolen goods.

"I ain't done nothin' wrong this time, Dave. I'll admit, some guy tried to sell me a stolen wildcat this morning, but I didn't wanna have nothin' to do with no snarling kitty-cat. The guy gave me this note in case I changed my mind, but it sure don't make no sense to me."

(¼   ?@+   #!!]   %@   ¼(#] $!

  (¢&c#   [!   )!&c¢½!]   &c%

%½!   [/&c¢=   !&c:/!   [@@=*%@)!

  @#   ¼@+)%½   *%)!!%

]@   #@%   *½@;   %½(*   #@%!

  %@   &c#?@#!   !/*!

                    $)   !

A = &c   D =]   R =)
B = [E = !   S = *
C = ¢   F = ¼   T = %

It's a good thing there's a partial key at the bottom. I'm sure that you can crack the code in no time.

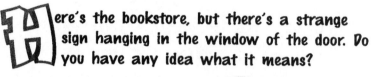 **H**ere's the bookstore, but there's a strange sign hanging in the window of the door. Do you have any idea what it means?

85

It's a good thing you figured out that sign! I asked the clerk if she knew where I could find Mr. E, but all she said was to put these books in alphabetical order, and then look at the middle word in each title. That seems pretty odd, but we might as well try it.

_____

_____

_____

_____

_____

_____

_____

_____

_____

_____

That must be the manager behind the counter.

"Mr. E? He's an old friend of mine. In fact, here's a map to his place. Just follow the directions and you'll be there in no time."

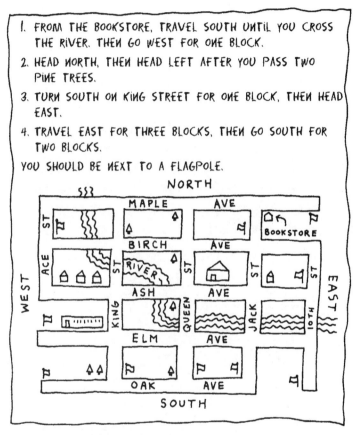

1. FROM THE BOOKSTORE, TRAVEL SOUTH UNTIL YOU CROSS THE RIVER. THEN GO WEST FOR ONE BLOCK.

2. HEAD NORTH, THEN HEAD LEFT AFTER YOU PASS TWO PINE TREES.

3. TURN SOUTH ON KING STREET FOR ONE BLOCK, THEN HEAD EAST.

4. TRAVEL EAST FOR THREE BLOCKS, THEN GO SOUTH FOR TWO BLOCKS.

YOU SHOULD BE NEXT TO A FLAGPOLE.

These directions are a little confusing. Would you circle the flagpole where we should end?

think we're in the right neighborhood, but the only person to help us find Mr. E's house is this little girl. She says that she'll tell us where Mr. E lives if we get her cat down from this tree. I'll give you a boost up, but make sure you get the right cat.

Mr. E lives in a house that looks exactly like mine. I'm not supposed to tell strangers where I live, but I *will* tell you that my house is on a corner of a block."

Gee, all of these houses on these two blocks look the same! Do *you* know which house the girl is talking about?

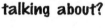

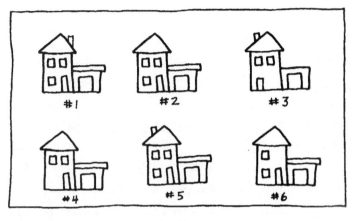

#1   #2   #3

#4   #5   #6

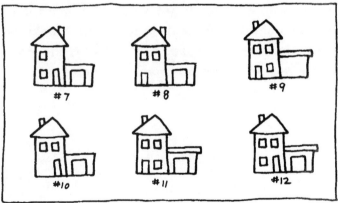

#7   #8   #9

#10   #11   #12

Uh-oh. Take a look at this sign on Mr. E's yard:

CAUTION

I've recently re-cemented the stones in my driveway. The blocks with an odd number of sides are still wet, and you'll get stuck in cement if you step on them. Please step only on the blocks with an even number of sides. And keep off the grass— it's where I keep my pet boa constrictor.

Can you find a safe path for us to follow? It would be a shame if we gave up now.

At last we've reached Mr. E, the person who stole the lynx. I can hear him coming to the door now.

Oh, no! I can't believe it! It's impossible! Mr. E is...

(To find out who Mr. E *is,* shade in all the spaces that contain the letter "E.")

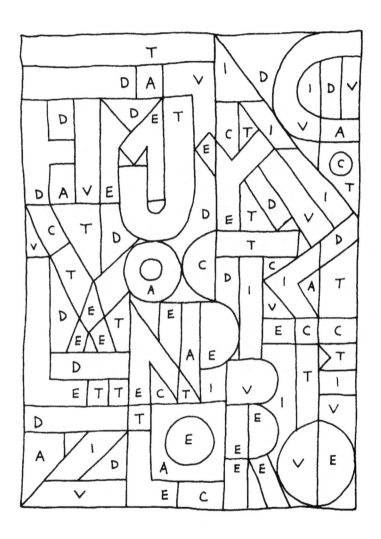

The police arrived immediately and arrested Mr. E, but I still don't understand why he stole the lynx in the first place. The police sergeant said Mr. E had given her this confusing confession. I'm worn out from all the work I've done today; why don't you figure out what it means.

DETE CTIVED AVEISS IXMO NTHSL ATEW
ITHHI SRENT. ITHO UGHTT HATIF ISTO
LETHEL YNXI TWO ULDBRI NGHIMSO
MEWOR KAN DHE WO ULDBEA BLETOP
AYME. IHO PEDTOS ELLT HECA TANDMA
KEAF EWEX TRABU CKSA SWELL. IINT
ENDED TOFRA MEJAKE. INE VERTH
OUGHTDE TEC TIVEDA VEWO ULDBES
MARTEN OUGHT OTRAC KMED OWN.

It's a good thing the missing lynx was in Mr. E's house. I guess that just about wraps up this case. I'm glad you had the opportunity to see me in action. My reward? To find out about that, I've got one last message for you to decode. Replace each letter below with the following letter of the alphabet: A = B, B = C, C = D,...Z = A. And feel welcome to stop by anytime you'd like. I always enjoy visiting with my admirers.

VGDM SGD KXMW VZR QDSTQMDC SN SGD

YNN, H VZR FHUDM DMNTFG LNMDX SN

OZX LX QDMS ENQ SGD MDWS EHUD

XDZQR.

A Dog Gone Dilemma

Howdy, puzzle-loving people! It's me again, Detective Dave. I'm glad you stopped by. It's been a slow day here in the detective business, but that never lasts. Pull up a chair; the phone never stays quiet for long. *Rrring!* Just a second, I'll be back as soon as I answer the telephone. . . .

Just *where* is that phone? I guess I should tidy up my office. Not only is this mess dangerous, I can't seem to find the phone! Can you find the cord that leads to where it is hidden?

That phone caller sure sounded desperate! She wants me to hurry to the La-De-Dah Estate. Why don't you come along for the ride? My cab driver friend, Maxi, can get us there in a flash. I'll get my notebook and pencil while you find her taxi. It doesn't look like any other cab in the city, so you'll be able to spot it in no time.

eepers! I've never seen so many roadblocks! Maxi is busy watching the traffic lights and I'm busy looking for my secret finger-printing tools in my detective bag, so you'd better direct us to the La-De-Dah Estate.

LA-DE-DAH ESTATE

lad we found the Estate so quickly. Maxi dropped us off at the front gate, but it's locked and there's no one around. The fence is too high to climb. Shouldn't there be a sign somewhere telling us where to go?

113

There's someone waiting for us at the back gate. It must be the woman who called me.

"Thank heavens you arrived, Detective Dave. My name is Martha. I'm Priscilla Van Astersloan III's maid. This meeting must be kept secret. To make certain no one overhears us, I've written down why I need your help."

pet Miss I feed Every poodle morning Astersloan's Van.

up When this Pierre was morning I woke gone!

away Pierre would run I never know.

him taken have must Someone.

show He is a big dog tomorrow in competing.

find as You must possible as him soon.

I can't find you job Pierre If my might lose.

Hmmm . . . this note doesn't make any sense. Perhaps Martha rearranged the words in each sentence to keep the message private, knowing that a pro like me would have no problem figuring out what it says. Let's see how *your* sleuth skills are: Unscramble the note.

Not bad for an amateur! While you figured that clue out, Martha handed me this photograph of Pierre so that we would be able to recognize him. It was taken at his last birthday party with his friends Fifi and Prince.

She told me that Fifi was looking at Pierre and admiring his new dog collar. Pierre had just eaten three bowls of ice cream, but he was not sitting next to Prince because Prince had spilled ice cream on him at his last party. Unfortunately I forgot to ask *which* dog was Pierre before Martha rushed back into the estate.

Can you tell which dog is which?

et's take a look around Pierre's doghouse for clues. Say, that's an unusual business card you've found. Too bad it's covered with scribbles. Perhaps if you follow the line connecting the two dots you'll still be able to read what it says.

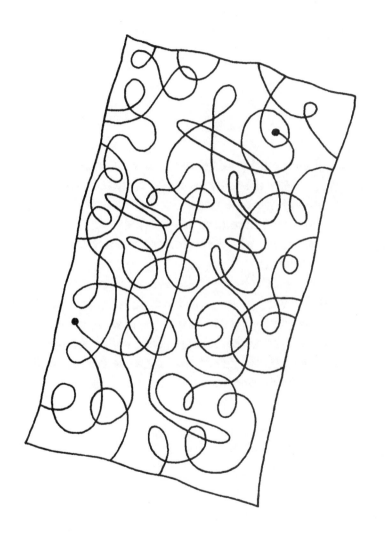

119

Good work! We'll begin our search there.
I showed my map to a passer-by and she said that in order to get to Oak Road, we should begin by heading south, and:

- ✔ turn east every time we pass a house with a chimney;
- ✔ turn south every time we pass a pine tree;
- ✔ turn west every time we pass a traffic light;
- ✔ turn north every time we cross a river.

When we come to a dead end, we're at our destination. These directions seem rather complicated to me. Perhaps you could trace our path for us.

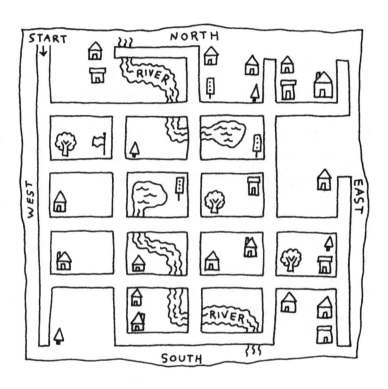

We're in luck! The first man we met on Oak Road said he saw a dog like Pierre in this apartment building. The dog was directly above a window with a flower pot, *not* next to a window with closed shutters, and either two windows to the left or to the right of a window with polka-dotted curtains.

Locate the window where the man saw the dog so we will know where to go.

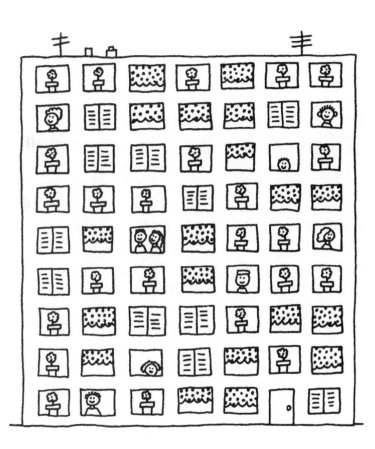

123

This elevator will take us up to the right floor. Maybe we'll find our dog!

Gee, that's an odd panel of buttons, but the other elevator riders didn't seem to have any trouble using it. One man said he wanted to go to the fourth floor and pushed the picture of the apple core. The other woman wanted to go to the ninth floor and pushed the pine tree.

We're the only ones left in the elevator. Which button do we push if we want to go the fifth floor?

We're on the right floor and this is the apartment we need to check, but the man who lives here won't open the door for us unless I can prove that I'm a real detective! He slid this piece of paper under the door and said that a true detective would be smart enough to figure out what it says.

Hurry! Help me read this message or we'll never find Pierre!

I 1 2 C

F U R YY.

¢ U R,

I L LET

U 2 N.

Uh-oh. When I showed that man the picture of Pierre and told him why we wanted to look in his apartment, he began to laugh. In fact, he's laughing so hard that he can't even talk, but he jotted down this note and handed it to me.

It looks like he left out all the O's in this message. Can you replace them and discover what he's trying to tell us?

WW! YU ARE FF CURSE
LKING IN UR HME FR YUR
LST PDLE. UR DG IS NLY
A CLTH TY FR UR TW -YEAR-
LD SN, BB! SRRY. DN'T
STP LKING, THUGH. G
DWN AK RAD NE BLCK
T UR TWN DG PUND.

That man gave us some good advice, but which of the four buildings on this block is the dog pound? Unfortunately there's no one around to ask.

One of these mailboxes must be labeled "DOG POUND," but it looks like the names are in some sort of code. If we knew which box was for the pound, we'd know which building to check. Can you determine which of these four mailboxes has the coded word "DOG POUND" on it?

ere's the dog pound! This note on the door seems rather unusual, but I guess we better follow the instructions if we want to get in.

Need help? Fit these dog breeds into this grid, then place the letters from the numbered boxes into the appropriate lines below.

PUG

CORGI
HUSKY

BEAGLE
COLLIE
SETTER
POODLE

SPANIEL
POINTER
MALTESE
MASTIFF
SAMOYED
WHIPPET

AIREDALE
MALAMUTE
DOBERMAN
PINSCHER

SCHNAUZER
PEKINGESE
GREYHOUND

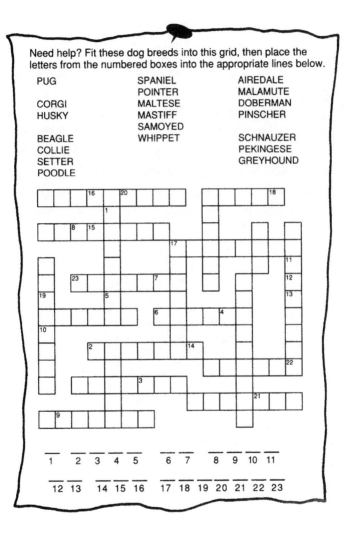

$\overline{}\ \overline{}\ \overline{}\ \overline{}\ \overline{}\quad \overline{}\ \overline{}\quad \overline{}\ \overline{}\ \overline{}\ \overline{}$
1   2   3   4   5   6   7   8   9   10 11

$\overline{}\ \overline{}\quad \overline{}\ \overline{}\ \overline{}\quad \overline{}\ \overline{}\ \overline{}\ \overline{}\ \overline{}\ \overline{}$
12 13   14 15 16   17 18 19 20 21 22 23

Just as you were finishing that puzzle, the dog catcher arrived!

"I see my note kept you busy while I went to get my lunch," he says. "I bet you're looking for a missing dog. I've got to go back to the deli for some mustard for my salami sandwich, but here are the lock combinations for the six kennels. You two are welcome to check them out for yourselves."

KENNEL LOCK COMBINATION

A : 2 - 4 - 6 - 8 - 10 - ___?___

B : 96 - 48 - 24 - 12 - 6 - ___?___

C : 12 - 24 - 36 - 48 - 60 - ___?___

D : 10 - 9 - 19 - 18 - 28 - ___?___

E : 43 - 36 - 29 - 22 - 15 - ___?___

F : 2 - 3 - 5 - 8 - 12 - ___?___

Oh, no! The last number is missing from each combination. Each set seems to be following some sort of pattern. Figure out the final number in each series while I figure out where I can get one of those salami sandwiches.

Drats! Pierre wasn't in any of the kennels. Where do we look now?

Hey! That suspicious-looking man who's hurrying by just dropped these two slips of paper. I've got a hunch! If we can figure out how they fit together, perhaps they will help us find Pierre.

T		M		H		V		T		E		A		T
	F		H		D		G		W		C		N	
H		P		H		M		U		O		T		E
	I		Y		O		I		H		A		D	
T		R		S		L		I		G		H		M
	O		O		R		W		E		P		H	
S		E		S		G		S		C		E		I
	A		T		H		S		E		L		O	
E		U		S		L		N		S		A		I

	O		I		A		E		H		L		S	
O		T		E		O		S		E		A		S
	I		T		E		O		T		F		H	
C		T		T		N		G		T		N		S
	A		T		E		L		N		T		E	
T		M		R		O		K		E		T		I
	M		S		A		E		E		R		T	
W		N		T		I		D		A		T		B
	O		R		A		O		E		H		R	

think we just uncovered a dog-stealing operation! Quick, follow that man! He headed across this cement parking lot. It would be bad luck if we stepped on a crack, so trace a path to the other side without crossing any of the lines.

He ducked into the building labeled "Warehouse 52," but the door is locked. We don't have time to try all these keys. Oh, poor Pierre! Which one should fit the door for Warehouse 52?

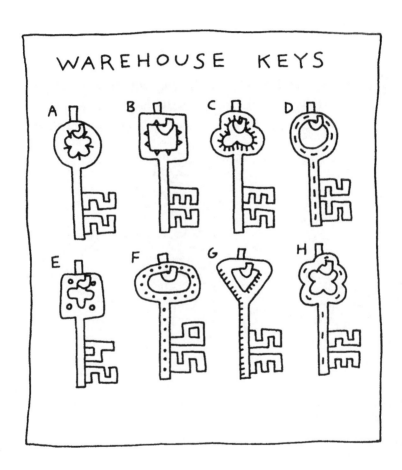

This unfinished sign in the warehouse next to these crates might be an important clue. You complete the sign while I look around for Pierre.

TOM, WE'LL NEED THIS SIGN IN ORDER FOR OUR PLAN TO
WORK. COLOR IN THE FOLLOWING SQUARES:

ROW Q: 3, 5, 7, 8, 10, 12, 14, 15
ROW M: 3, 5, 7, 8, 10, 11, 12, 14, 15
ROW E: 4, 6, 8, 9, 10, 13
ROW H: 2, 4, 6, 8, 10, 15
ROW J: 2, 4, 6, 8, 10, 13, 17
ROW O: 3, 4, 5, 7, 8, 10, 11, 14, 15
ROW B: 4, 6, 8, 10, 13
ROW I: 2, 4, 6, 8, 10, 12, 13, 15, 16, 17
ROW P: 3, 5, 7, 10, 12, 14
ROW K: 2, 3, 6, 7, 8, 10, 11, 12, 13, 15, 16, 17
ROW D: 4, 6, 8, 10, 13
ROW N: 3, 5, 7, 10, 12, 14
ROW G: 2, 3, 6, 7, 8, 10, 11, 15, 16, 17
ROW A: 4, 6, 8, 9, 10, 12, 13, 14
ROW C: 4, 5, 6, 8, 10, 13

LOVE,
SHARI

	1	2	3	4	5	6	7	8	9	10	11	12	13	14	15	16	17	18
A																		
B																		
C																		
D																		
E																		
F																		
G																		
H																		
I																		
J																		
K																		
L																		
M																		
N																		
O																		
P																		
Q																		

Those crates were full of frankfurters and buns! It looks like Tom and Shari weren't selling stolen pooches after all!

But where is *Pierre*!

Hey, did you hear that? When I shouted "Pierre!" I heard a bark coming from that building across the street. Let's investigate. . . .

What is this place? It looks like the letters have fallen off the building's sign. Put them back in their proper places so we'll know where we're heading.

There's Pierre! He's being carried out of the building by that woman wearing all sorts of fancy jewelry.

"Why, you must be Detective Dave. My name is Priscilla Van Astersloan III. My maid, Martha, said that I might see you here. She wanted me to give you this note, though she wouldn't say why. Toodle-oo! I simply *must* be on my way!"

Wvgvxgrev Wzev,

  Zh hllm zh blf ovug R
ivnvnyvivw gszg Nrhh Ezm
Zhgviholzm dzh tlrmt gl gzpv
Krviiv rmgl gsv kvg hzolm uli z
hsznkll zmw szrixfg. R zn hliib
gl szev ylgsvivw blf.

           Nzigsz

Oh well, the day wasn't a complete loss for me. I was able to get something I needed at the end of our search. To find out what, circle the word in each group that does not belong, then read all of your circled answers.

1. heel   toe   eye   sole

2. saw   mop   broom   sponge

3. Ned   Pete   Ted   Fred

4. and   star   tars   rats

5. yesterday now   past   ago

6. whole   half   total   all

7. f   k   A   e

8. swam   jumped   knew   ran

9. camel   horse   hare   mule

10. connect join   unite   cut

Trapped in Hill House!

Hello, puzzle fans! Yes, it's me, the one and only Detective Dave, fearless and famed master of mysteries. I'm glad you stopped by. Let me check my mailbox, then we can go inside and I'll tell you all about my latest and greatest crime-stopping accomplishments. . . .

Drats! The neighbor's cat has gotten into my mail again and has torn up these two letters. Perhaps you could carefully look at the pieces and tell me what the letters should say.

155

One of the letters sounded important. We'd better investigate.

My car is a little low on gas, so we'll take my tandem bicycle–it's built for two. What do you think of my specially designed bike lock? To open it, I just rotate the four dials so that they spell the secret password. Unfortunately I keep forgetting what the word is. However I do remember that it's an animal. I'll let you discover the password while I pump up the tires.

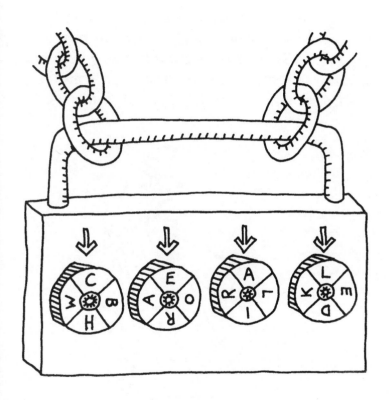

157

Here's the house. Gee, it's not very welcoming. The sign says we must pay 25¢ to open each gate, and I only have a dollar in change. Can you find a path to the front door that passes through just four gates?

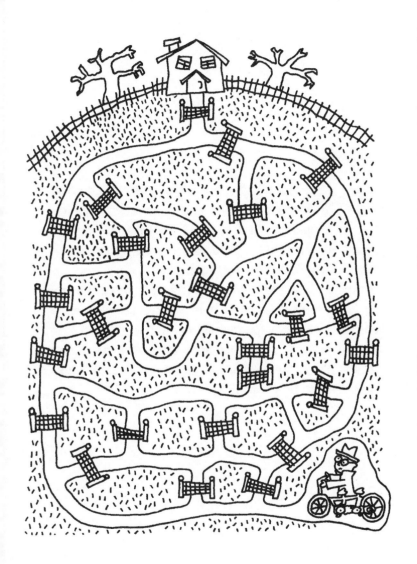

Good work! I'll ring the doorbell—Yeeow! When I pressed the buzzer a trapdoor opened, and we slid down a chute to a pile of hay in this locked cage! What are we going to do? How will we ever get out?

Hmm . . . it looks like somebody erased some of the letters on that note you found. The message doesn't look very encouraging, but maybe the missing letters are some sort of a clue as to what we should do next. You fill them in; I'm still shaking from the fall!

HA! YOU ARE _RAPPED
IN _ERE FOR_VER.
T_YING TO _SCAPE _S
U_ELESS. THESE B_RS
ARE UNBREA_ABL_.
_OU S_OULD G_VE
UP HOPE IMME_IATELY.
_ON'T _VEN THI_K OF
LEAV__G; T_IS C_GE
IS NOW _OUR HOME!

Once you found the clue in that note, getting out of the cage was a snap! But where do we go now? I don't see any doors. In fact, there's not much in this room except for that big, old bookcase. Whoever owns this place doesn't do a very good job of keeping the books in order. I bet there's a secret door behind the bookcase, but it's too heavy to push. I wish there was a clue as to how to get out, but I can't find one . . . can you?

163

Yikes! The opening behind the bookcase led to this bat-filled cave! Find the path out of here without touching any of the bats as quickly as possible.

Ick! I don't like the way they're looking at me!

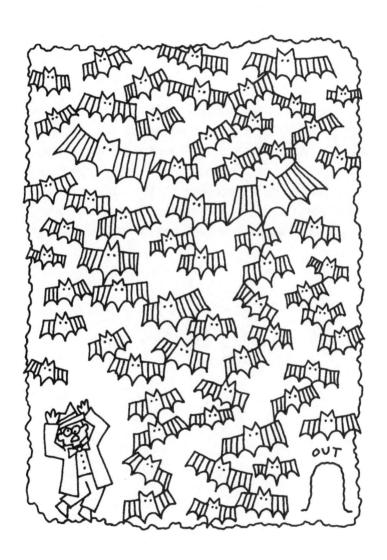

These cave tunnels twist and turn so much that I have no idea where we are. I'm worried that we'll never get out of here! That's odd! Look at that odd-looking spider and the odd way he's watching us. It's almost as if he's trying to tell us something. Connect his web using only the *odd* numbers and see what happens.

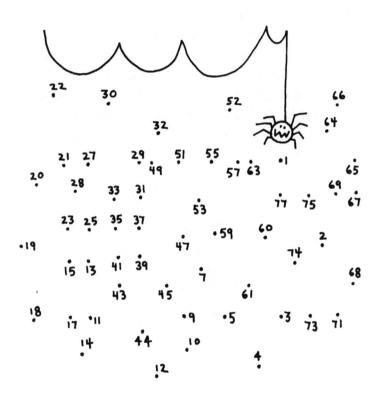

Good thing we found that spider or we might still be lost!

Oh no, now what?! This room is beginning to fill with water . . . and all the doors are locked! Quick, I've got an idea: Find the three keys whose total equals one of the door numbers. That must be the way to unlock the door. And hurry, I don't think I can hold my breath for very long!

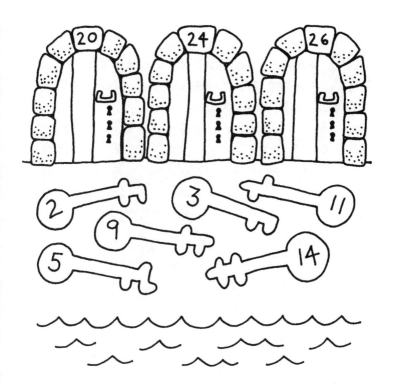

Whew! That was close! But I don't think we're out of danger yet. Look at the sign on this wall:

The floor to this room is rigged with traps. To leave safely, you must step on every square just once, moving up and down or across—but not diagonally. If you find the correct path, you'll also spell out a hidden message. Otherwise it's curtains for you!

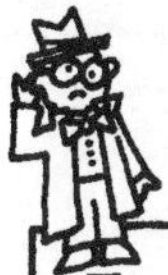

You take the lead on this one.
I'm sure you can do it in no time!

I	F	I	S	P	U
O	Y	H	T	Z	Z
U	I	N	K	L	E
T	H	H	S	A	W
O	T	A	U	S	T
S	D	R	J	A	W
O	L	V	E	I	T

EXIT

We've reached an underground river. I wonder why there are so many bridges across it. We'd better read this sign and think carefully before we choose which bridge to cross:

WARNING!

Only one of these bridges is sturdy enough to hold a person's weight.

- The safe bridge is not next to a bridge made of an even number of boards.

- The safe bridge is built of more boards than at least one of the two bridges it is between.

- The safe bridge has the same number of boards as at least one other bridge.

Hmm . . . so many bridges to choose from. Can you figure this one out?

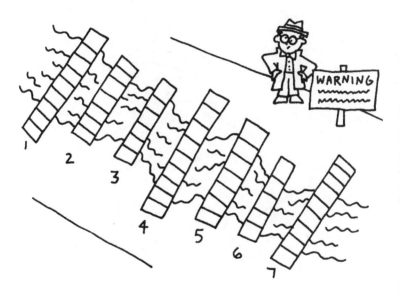

2 knew you'd pick the right bridge! Let's just cross to the other side and—whoa! Where did that nasty-looking alligator come from?

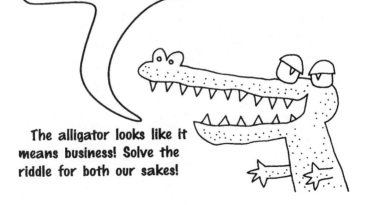

You cannot cross my bridge, unless
This riddle's answer you can guess:

First find an insect that flies with its wings,
    Travels to flowers, and frequently stings;
Second you'll need what a needle has, too,
    A potato has many, there's two found on you;
Third take a drink that is served iced or hot,
    Sipped from a cup, and is poured from a pot;
The last is a letter quite easy to seek,
    You will find it four times in "EVERY WEEK."

Together they spell out what I like to do,
If you don't know the answer, I'LL DO THIS TO YOU!

The alligator looks like it means business! Solve the riddle for both our sakes!

Good guess! I was just about to say the same thing myself. Perhaps this door over here will be the way out of this creepy old place.

I don't understand. I've pushed the red button on this electric door opener. Why won't the door open?

177

Now that the door is open, it looks like we've found someone who hopefully can show us the way out.

"Come in, my pretties. I'd love to help you! But first I need some assistance with this special alphabet stew I'm brewing. Shade in all the letters found in the magic word **MIZWRX**, then read what's left in my cauldron."

IS HIM Z CRIM
PRAW BRAXORY
AWE SIJ ERSIN OX
WILZ MUXE T IMU
LIX SINIR
RIT

Give a helping hand with the stew while I add another dash of "eye of newt."

POOF! What's going on? As soon as I read those words, the woman disappeared in a cloud of smoke, and look what happened to me! Hurry, color in all the triangles to see what I've turned into!

Oh, this is terrible! I'll never be able to continue my detective work in this condition. You've got to help me get back to my wonderful, normal self. That scroll on the table might give us a hint as to how I can change back, but I can't read that crazy writing, can you?

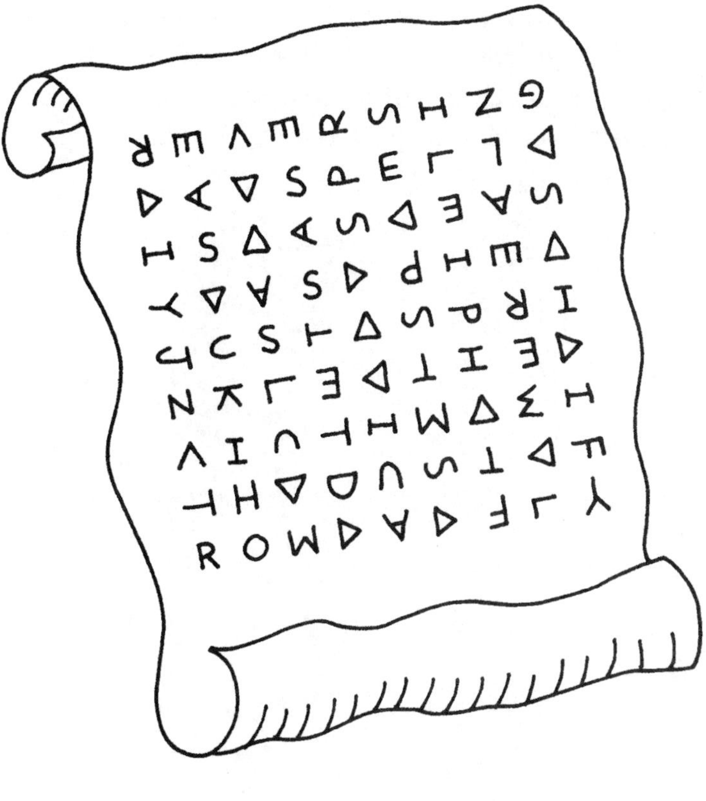

Perhaps the cupboard has the ingredient we need. Just our luck, it's locked! Here's a set of keys, but if this note is correct, we'd better be sure to pick the right one.

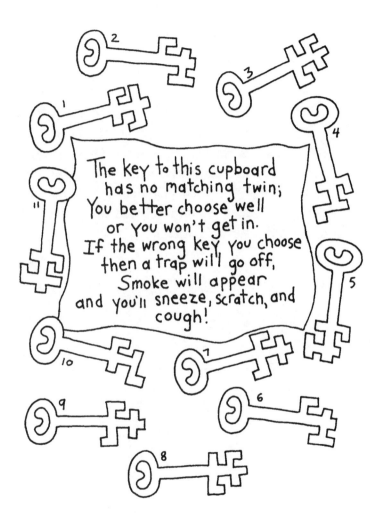

The key to this cupboard
has no matching twin;
You better choose well
or you won't get in.
If the wrong key you choose
then a trap will go off,
Smoke will appear
and you'll sneeze, scratch, and
cough!

reat job! We opened the cupboard safely, but how can we tell which of these bottles contains "fly dust"? Those strange markings on the bottles must mean something, but I'm completely baffled. Can you figure this one out? Hurry! In my present condition those insects are starting to look tasty to me!

186

Hooray! That fly dust did the trick! Once again, I'm as handsome as ever!

Uh-oh. The door to this room has vanished! What are we going to do now? Wait a minute, there's a hole behind these boards. Maybe this is the way out. . . .

Oops, I guess I should have read the writing on the boards before I moved them. Can you put them in order so that they spell out a message? I'm afraid to go in there unless we know that it is safe.

189

The passageways behind the boards curl over and under so much that I'm getting dizzy just looking at them. You had better lead us out of this one.

191

We're almost outside! I can see daylight coming from that hole in the ceiling! But how will we ever reach it? The hole is just too high up, and it's being guarded by a vicious-looking snake that's rattling its tail.

Hey, it looks like you found another interesting note. I wonder if it'll help. What can you make of it?

How to turn a rattlesnake into something useful

R A T T L E S N A K E

_____

_____

_____

_____

_____

_____

1. Change all the E's to A's and all the A's to E's.

2. Reverse the positions of the fifth and sixth letters.

3. Change all the T's to D's.

4. Cross out the last letter and move the seventh letter to that position.

5. Change the N to P and change the K to T.

6. Write all the letters in reverse order.

Hot dog! We were able to climb through the hole and finally escape that awful place! Say, I wonder who that strange man approaching us is?

"Detective Dave! I was afraid you wouldn't come. The second page of my letter got jammed in my printer and did not get mailed. The computer mistakenly added one letter to the beginning or the end of each word, but I'm sure you can still read it. Then you'll know exactly why I needed your help."

IN SHAVE AS BRANDY NEWT FUND
HOUSED BRIDE EAT AMY THEMED
SPARK, ABUT IT DOG NOTE WANTS
SIT TOP BED TOOL CHAIR-RAISING
FORK LITTLER SKIDS. IS KNOWN
YOUR CARE THEM FRIGHT ZONE
TOE TESTY HIT POUT FORM MEN.

Detective Dave's help proves to be invaluable once again! I knew all along that we were never in any real danger. I may have looked scared, but I just wanted to see whether your puzzle-solving skills were as sharp as mine. Nonetheless, you can keep what that man gave me for helping him. It's written in code, but he told me the first words are THANK YOU.

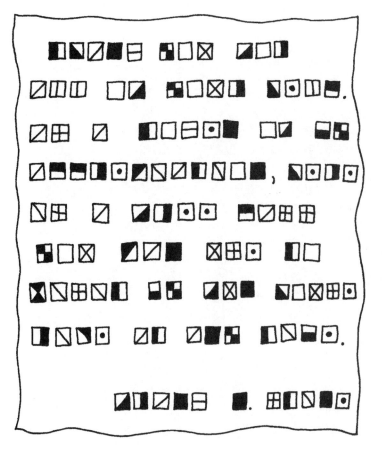

Detective Dave's Bummer Vacation

Maybe it's a good thing I ran into you here. I'm on my way to catch my airplane, but I can't remember the flight number. I jotted it down on a slip of paper and stuck it in my coat pocket, but unfortunately my pocket was already filled with other notes. I remember that my flight number looked the same even if read upside-down. Would you mind helping me find the right slip of paper?

Thanks! I see you've noticed my suitcase. It belonged to my grandmother, Detective Dora. She traveled all over the world. Each label is supposed to represent one of the countries she visited, but I could never understand them. Can you tell where Grandma Dora has been?

205

While you were studying my suitcase I bumped into a suspicious-looking woman. She reminded me of someone I saw on a poster. In fact, I think I have a copy of that poster in my pants pocket. OOPS! It looks like the poster got chewed up when my pants went through the washer. Copy the pieces into their correct places on the grid, then we can both check out the poster.

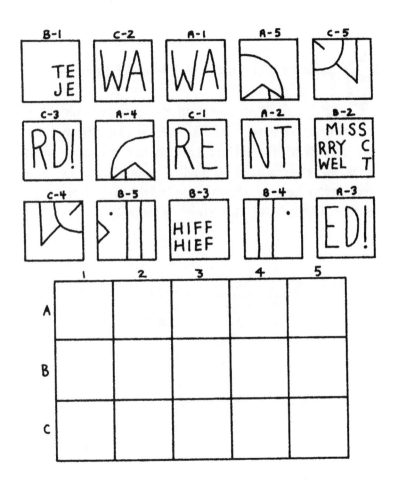

That's the woman I bumped into! Quick, after her!

A little boy said he saw her jump into a taxi. He wouldn't tell me which one, though. He did say that the letters on the taxi's license plate could be rearranged to spell at least five different five-letter words. Hurry and select the right taxi before Miss Chiff has time to escape!

209

Fiddlesticks! Her taxi is driving away. Grab another cab and we'll follow her.

Boy, it seems like they're making these freeways more complicated all the time. I'll try not to get carsick if you help our cab driver catch up to Miss Chiff's taxi.

The cab dropped off Miss Chiff at this train station, but I can't find her anywhere. A security guard said he saw Miss Chiff pick up a brochure, carelessly put it back on the rack, then rush for a train. Hmmm. If we knew which brochure Miss Chiff looked at, we might know where she was headed. Do any of these brochures look out of order to you?

TRAVEL BROCHURES

ANTAPOLIS

VISIT BAKER CITY

CLEAR BAY A PLACE TO STAY

EVERYONE LOVES DOG TOWN

East End IS EXCITING!

frogville

see historic HAPPY HOLLOW

ICEVILLE IS NICE!

RELAX AT JUNE CREEK

KING CITY TREATS YOU LIKE ROYALTY

LAKELAND

MOON HILL A SWELL CITY

COME TO NEWPORT

see OAK RIDGE

GARDEN GROVE IS GREAT!

PINE COVE

Nicely done! That must be where she is headed. Unfortunately, the last train of the day just left.

Say, that's an interesting poster you've noticed. Perhaps it could be useful to us. Too bad someone scribbled extra letters over it. Here's an idea: I'll use my magnifying glass to determine which letters are fake, and you cross them out.

CAREFREEZING
SHOTELAIRKS
BASEBALLOONEY
BRIDESMAID
STODAYBRAINED
OTHERSPARKLING

Cross out:
* The last two letters in line 2, line 3, and line 5.
* The 7th, 8th, and 9th letters in line 5.
* The first letter in line 2, line 4, line 5, and line 6.
* The last four letters in line 1, line 4, and line 6.
* The 5th and 6th letters in line 2 and line 6.
* The first four letters in line 1 and line 3.

Way to go! That's how we'll get to the next city.

The sign says that Tyrone is giving free balloon rides today, but which balloon is his? They all look the same to me. See if you can find a balloon that matches the sign. I'm going to catch a quick nap on this park bench.

ood job finding Tyrone's balloon. I sure hope he can help us out....

"Sure, I'd be happy to give you two a free ride," Tyrone says, "but first you'll have to give me a hand. I accidentally tore my latest balloon permit. The festival officials won't let me take off without it. The two halves are somewhere in my flight pouch, along with leftover permits from past years. The valid license spells BALLOON PERMIT. Can you see which two pieces I need?"

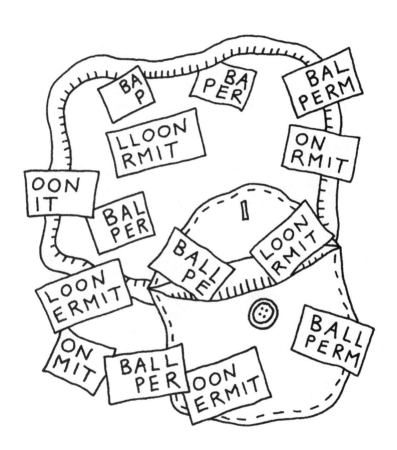

Now that Tyrone has his complete permit, we are ready to take off. It shouldn't be long before we're flying over our destination. Tyrone says there will be a sign pointing to the landing field.

Yikes! We sure are high up in the air! I'd rather not open my eyes until we're on the ground. You'd better find the sign.

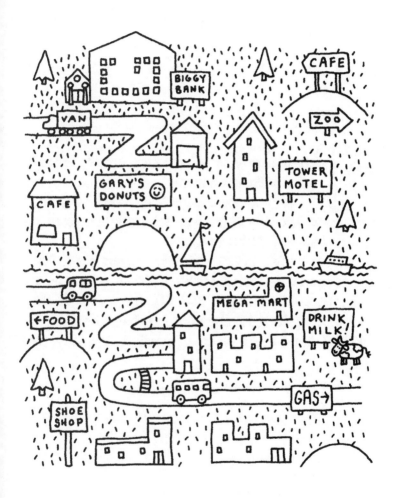

221

Thanks to your sharp eyes, Tyrone landed the balloon perfectly.

Oh no! There goes Miss Chiff on that bus! Let's ask the ticket agent at the bus depot where BUS #36 is headed.

"I wish I could help," the ticket agent says, "but our computer is malfunctioning. When I type in our company's name: 1-2-3 BUS CO. the screen displays A-B-C 2-21-19 3-15. Here's a print-out of today's schedule, but I doubt whether it will do you any good."

4-5-19-20-9-14-1-20-9-15-14 (DESTINATION)	2-21-19 14-21-13-2-5-18 (BUS NUMBER)
19-16-18-9-14-7-6-9-5-12-4	A-B
2-12-21-5 22-1-12-12-5-25	F-D
20-5-5-14-25 20-15-23-14	D-H
2-12-1-2-2-5-18-2-21-18-7	C-G
18-9-22-5-18 3-9-20-25	C-F
13-5-7-1-22-9-12-12-5	E-A

Hmmmm. There must be a way to decode this mess and discover where BUS #36 is headed. Any ideas?

Now we know where Miss Chiff is headed! I'm afraid I'm a little low on cash. Pick the cheapest way the two of us can get to River City.

1 didn't realize our route to River City would take us through such a winding forest. Our driver said to pay attention to the billboards we pass. The letters on them will spell out a place we should be certain to visit in town.

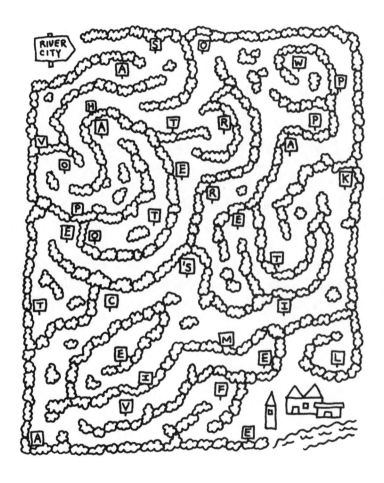

227

It's a good thing we stopped here. Kim said Miss Chiff was in here five minutes ago. She asked Kim to mail this postcard to her mother for her. I know it's not polite to read other people's mail, but this might be just the clue we need to nab that thief.

It figures! That sneaky Miss Chiff used a code to write her message. My guess is that the first word is "DEAR." Now that I've decoded the most difficult part, you decode the rest of this postcard to Miss Chiff's mom.

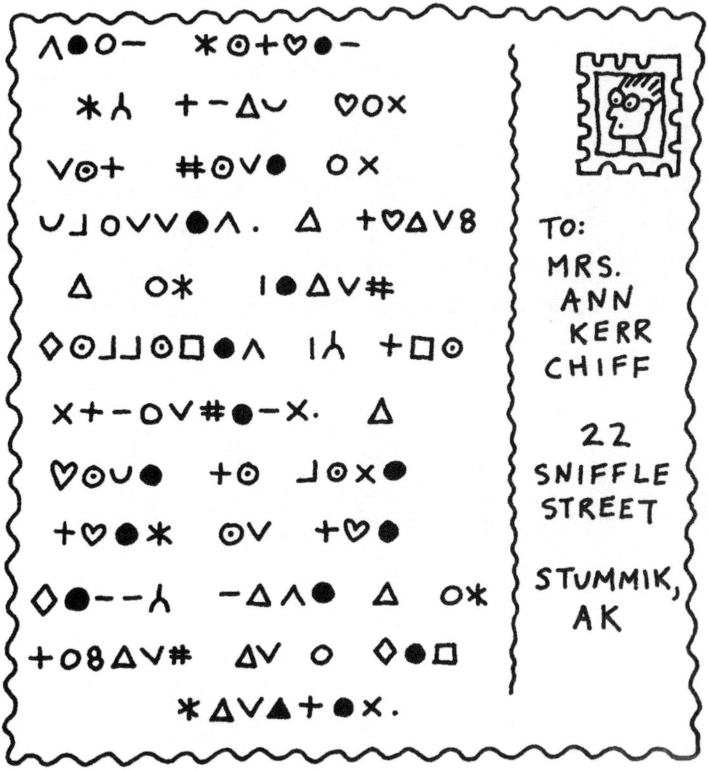

TO:
MRS.
ANN
KERR
CHIFF

22
SNIFFLE
STREET

STUMMIK,
AK

was sure we would catch Miss Chiff at the ferry, but we're too late again...or maybe not! The ferry is just pulling away now. I bet one of these boats is tied to the ferry. If we jump into the right one, we'll get pulled across the river, and I'll arrest Miss Chiff on the other side. I'll leave it up to you to pick the boat. Don't delay!

Not again! Miss Chiff was already gone by the time we got out of the boat! The ferry captain said he saw her go into his uncle Pat's store across the street. Maybe she's still there. Gee, I wonder which store the captain was talking about.

233

Yes, indeed," the clerk tells us. "A woman fitting that description was just in here. She bought three souvenirs, one from each row. She gave me a $20 bill, and I gave her $2 change. Then she ran out, hopped onto a rented motorbike, and rode away."

If we determine what she bought, it might help us determine where she's off to now. Use your math skills to figure out what Miss Chiff purchased while I check out the shop's nifty supply of detective tools.

Good thinking! All those souvenirs are probably from the town she is going to next. This biker says she'll drive us there on her motorcycle. How exciting! I've never ridden in a sidecar before! She warned, however, that repair crews are replacing the telephone wires by connecting poles with matching letters. It would be safer if we did not pass underneath those wires. Don't worry about the poles without a match, but see if there is still a safe route from here to the next town.

Look! There's Miss Chiff! She stopped in front of that sign, then headed in the opposite direction that the arrow is pointing. Even though it looks like it's written in a foreign language, that sign is probably another important clue. You had better read it before we continue chasing her.

miles
one
→
uui
apishuuns

That sign *was* important. The desk clerk at the inn said Miss Chiff just checked in, but no matter how much I begged, he refused to tell me which room is hers. Now what do we do?

I see you've found some interesting scraps in the wastebasket. Is it possible that they all form a message?

OUTSIDE OF ROOM

SMITH. THERE SHOULD BE

20. THANKS.

2. THEY WON'T BE HEAVY. THEN

BELLHOP~ DON'T FORGET TO

CHIFF WHO IS IN ROOM

BRING A CUP OF TEA TO MISS

8. THEY BELONG TO MISS

PICK UP THE SUITCASES

This is terrible! As soon as you unscrambled that note, I dashed up to Miss Chiff's room to arrest her, but after all my hard work it seems I won't be getting a reward after all. I'm too embarrassed to tell you why, but if you're as clever as I think you are, you can easily discover the answer. Starting with the first letter, read every other letter in this note I've written. Then go back and read the remaining letters.

```
T  I  H  T  E  W  W  A  O  S  M
H  A  E  N  R  W  I  E  D  W  E
E  N  R  T  E  I  F  C  O  A  L
L  L  T  O  W  W  I  I  N  N  S
G  I  W  S  A  T  S  E  N  R  O
M  T  I  M  S  I  S  S  S  S  H
T  E  E  R  R  R  R  I  Y  C
C  H  H  I  I  F  F  F  F
```

That about winds up this case. I'd like to go back to the airport, catch another plane, and start my vacation over—except for one problem. To learn what my final challenge is, circle my name, DAVE, every time it appears in the grid of letters below. Hint: my name is hidden 28 times.

244

```
V  A  D  E  P  A  D  E  V  A  D  M  D  L  T  R  P  L  D  V
Q  S  A  B  Z  N  D  V  G  O  A  H  A  A  M  J  K  A  A  M
O  U  V  K  B  I  A  A  B  O  V  A  V  B  V  Z  V  H  V  T
K  M  E  W  N  T  A  D  A  V  E  N  E  M  A  E  S  C  E  O
X  E  V  S  H  A  V  A  P  Q  V  M  V  I  C  T  R  D  V  U
N  R  A  Q  T  C  V  V  M  O  A  I  A  R  C  Q  R  U  A  K
N  P  D  Y  Q  A  E  E  Z  K  D  S  D  E  A  V  U  S  D  U
B  U  M  E  R  V  P  U  Z  E  L  T  T  R  T  H  W  D  P  L
D  P  K  L  M  N  O  P  D  A  V  E  Z  D  A  V  E  V  A  D
A  N  J  D  A  V  E  Q  D  N  D  R  U  N  Z  F  V  V  A  D
V  Q  I  A  W  X  V  R  K  A  K  Y  N  L  E  H  A  E  E  T
E  Q  H  V  V  U  A  S  N  N  V  K  P  C  C  K  D  R  D  I
V  U  G  E  V  A  D  T  D  E  L  E  T  I  V  E  A  G  W  N
A  N  F  E  D  C  B  A  E  V  A  D  C  H  P  O  V  I  O  G
D  A  V  E  Y  Z  K  Z  E  F  G  K  D  P  H  K  E  H  H  S
```

245

ANSWERS

Page 11:

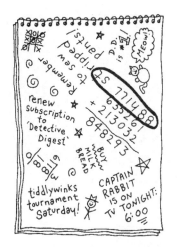

Page 13:

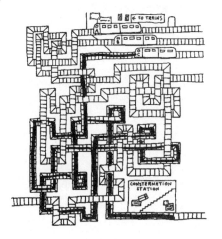

Page 15:

Page 17:

The elevator works by pushing the
buttons that form the shape of the floor
number. For example, the buttons, B, E,
H, K, N make the shape of number one.
To get to the fifth floor, push C, B, A, D,
G, H, I, L, O, N, M.

Page 19:

The doors are labeled with rebuses.

501   Doris Carson
        (door + S car + sun)

502   Jack Fisher
        (jack fish + er)

503   Carmen Applebee
        (car + men apple + bee)

504   Andy Bowman
        (and + E bow + man)

Starting at the "A" in the center of the grid and spiraling outward counter-clockwise, the description reads:

After years of difficult work, I have finally discovered a way to make someone invisible. My invention is a suit of invisible clothes. Whoever wears the suit completely disappears from view. It is, without a doubt, my greatest invention ever.

Page 23:

Connecting the points in order reveals a picture of the Science Museum.

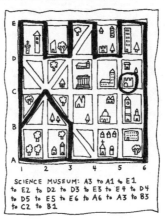

SCIENCE MUSEUM: A3 to A1 to E1 to E2 to D2 to D3 to E3 to E4 to D4 to D5 to E5 to E6 to A6 to A3 to B3 to C2 to B1

Page 25:

Great Inventor's Auditorium

The doors must open outward (according
to the placement of the hinges). The
first, second, and fourth doors have
objects in front of them that would have
been disturbed had they been opened.
The thief must have escaped through the
door marked "KEEP OUT."

Page 29:

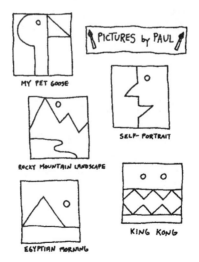

Page 35:

Page 37:

There are 114 bricks in the gate. Two
admissions would cost $2.28.

Page 39:

The signs should read:
KEEP OFF THE GRASS
BIKE PATH
NO SWIMMING IN THE LAKE
TO PICNIC TABLES
PARK CLOSES AT MIDNIGHT
KEEP OUR PARK CLEAN

Page 41:

Page 43:

Clue B states the fourth digit is more
than 7, and since there are no 8s in the
answer (Clue C), the fourth digit must be
9. The second digit is four less than the
fourth digit (Clue D), so it must be 5.
The sixth digit is 2 (Clue E). Either the
first three or last three digits are the
same (Clue A). The last three digits can't
be the same (Clue F), so the first three
digits must be five. One of the remaining
digits is 6, then the sum of the fifth and
sixth digit (Clue F) would equal 8, but
there are no 8s in the answer. Therefore
the seventh digit must be 6. Since the
sum of the fifth and sixth digits equals 6
(Clue F), the fifth digit must be 4.

Yes, I stole Dr. Carson's invisible suit. I
am a school principal and I am always
the one who has to punish students who
misbehave. I thought if I was invisible, it
would give me the chance to misbehave
for once.

The code phonetically spells out this
message:

H-E H-A-S T-O C-L-E-A-N T-H-E
S-C-H-O-O-L L-U-N-C-H-R-O-O-M F-O-R
O-N-E W-H-O-L-E Y-E-A-R!

255

Page 59:

IF YOU ARE CLEVER ENOUGH TO
DECODE THIS NOTE, THEN PERHAPS
YOU WILL BE ABLE TO HELP ME. PLEASE
COME AT ONCE TO THE CITY ZOO.
SOMETHING TERRIBLE HAS HAPPENED.

Page 61:

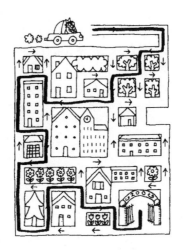

Page 63:

Zoo Director TOM HERNANDEZ

Feeding Supervisor JANICE JONES

Secretary TERRY WASHINGTON

Head of Security TINA JACKSON

Gardener THEODORE ERICKSON

256

Page 65:

LAST NIGHT AFTER THE
ZOO HAD CLOSED A
THIEF SNUCK INTO THE
WILD CAT BUILDING
AND STOLE THE ZOO'S
NEW LYNX.

Page 67:

Jennifer must be lying.

If Jennifer were telling the truth, then
both Jackie and Jamal would be lying.
This cannot be the case, since only *one*
guard is not telling the truth.

Page 69:

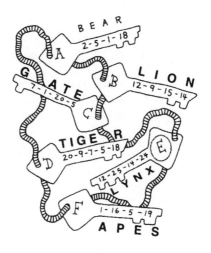

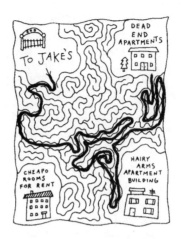

Jake lives in apartment #5.

The speaker lives in apartment #1. Mr. Wagner lives on one side of him, in apartment #2. Mrs. Wu lives on the other side of Mr. Wagner in apartment #3. Mrs. Wu does not live next door to Jake, so Jake must not live in apartment #4. The only apartment left is #5.

Page 75:

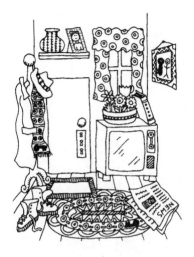

Page 77:

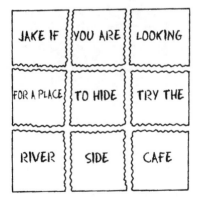

JAKE IF	YOU ARE	LOOKING
FOR A PLACE	TO HIDE	TRY THE
RIVER	SIDE	CAFE

Page 79:

The capital letters in the menu spell out the message:

TRAP DOOR UNDER RUG.

Page 81:

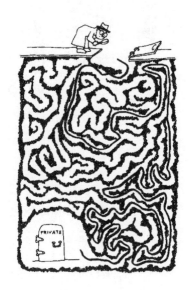

Page 83:

IF YOU NEED TO FIND ME
I CAN BE REACHED AT
THE BLACK EAGLE BOOKSTORE
ON FOURTH STREET.
DO NOT SHOW THIS NOTE
TO ANYONE ELSE.

MR. E

Page 85:

The sign was put up backwards.
When viewed in a mirror it reads:

CAUTION: WET PAINT
USE BACK DOOR

Page 87:

ABBY AND ANDREW (ASK) THE BIG QUESTION

BENEATH (THE) OCEAN

CANDY (STORE) RECIPES

CHOOSING THE BEST (MANAGER) FOR THE TEAM

MONSTERS (AND) MYSTERIES

PICASSO: IS (HE) REALLY DEAD?

WASHINGTON'S LAST (WILL) AND TESTAMENT

WHO WILL (HELP) THE WHALES?

WHY (YOU) SLEEP

(ANSWER)
ASK THE STORE MANAGER AND HE
WILL HELP YOU

Page 89:

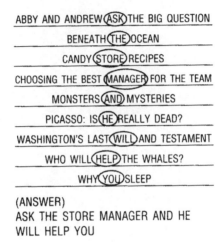

#5 and #12 are identical. Since #12 is on a corner then Mr. E must live in house #5.

Page 97:

Page 99:

By respacing the letters,
the message reads:

DETECTIVE DAVE IS SIX MONTHS LATE
WITH HIS RENT. I THOUGHT THAT IF I
STOLE THE LYNX IT WOULD BRING HIM
SOME WORK AND HE WOULD BE ABLE
TO PAY ME. I HOPED TO SELL THE CAT
AND MAKE A FEW EXTRA BUCKS AS
WELL. I INTENDED TO FRAME JAKE. I
NEVER THOUGHT DETECTIVE DAVE
WOULD BE SMART ENOUGH TO TRACK
ME DOWN.

Page 101:

WHEN THE LYNX WAS RETURNED TO
THE ZOO, I WAS GIVEN ENOUGH
MONEY TO PAY MY RENT FOR THE
NEXT FIVE YEARS.

The phone is in the bucket.

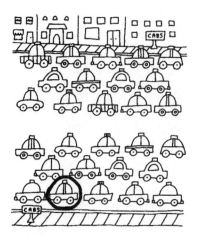

Page 111:

Page 113:

The letters in the gate, reading downward,
spell "VISITORS SHOULD USE THE REAR
GATE."

After rearranging the words, the
sentences read:
Every morning I feed Miss Van
Astersloan's pet poodle.
When I woke up this morning Pierre
was gone!
I know Pierre would never run away.
Someone must have taken him.
He is competing in a big dog show
tomorrow.
You must find him as soon as possible.
If you can't find Pierre I might lose my
job.

From left to right, the dogs are Pierre,
Fifi, and Prince.
Pierre and Prince are not sitting next to
each other, so Fifi must be the dog in the
middle. Fifi is looking at Pierre's collar,
so Pierre must be the dog on the left.

The line connecting the two dots spells
"OAK ROAD."

Page 121:

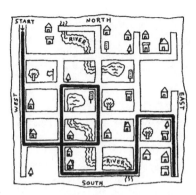

Page 123:

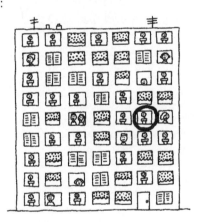

Page 125:

For the fifth floor, push the hive.
The buttons are labeled with pictures that
rhyme with the different floor numbers:

one=sun	two=shoe	three=key
four=core	five=hive	six=chicks
seven=eleven	eight=skate	nine=pine

Pronouncing the letters, numbers, and
symbols aloud, the message reads:
I WANT TO SEE IF YOU ARE WISE.
SINCE YOU ARE, I'LL LET YOU TWO IN.

The message reads:
WOW, YOU ARE OFF COURSE LOOKING
IN OUR HOME FOR YOUR LOST
POODLE. OUR DOG IS ONLY A CLOTH
TOY FOR OUR TWO-YEAR-OLD SON,
BOB! SORRY. DON'T STOP LOOKING.
THOUGH. GO DOWN OAK ROAD ONE
BLOCK TO OUR TOWN DOG POUND.

The dog pound is BUILDING C.
The coded words "DOG POUND" must
be three and five symbols long each. The
first symbol of the first word,
representing the D in "DOG," must be the
same as the last symbol of the second
word, representing the D in "POUND."
Likewise, the second symbol of both
words, representing the letter O, also
must be the same. Only the code on the
mailbox for BUILDING C fits this pattern.

The numbered boxes spell out:
I WILL BE BACK IN TEN MINUTES.

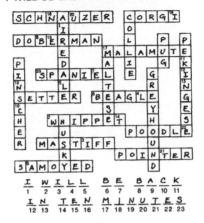

A: 2-4-6-8-10-**12**
(add two to each number)
B: 96-48-24-12-6-**3**
(divide each number by two)
C: 12-24-36-48-60-**72**
(add twelve to each number)
D: 10-9-19-18-28-**27**
(subtract one, add ten, subtract one, add ten, etc.)
E: 43-36-29-22-15-**8**
(subtract seven from each number)
F: 2-3-5-8-12-**17**
(add one, add two, add three, etc.)

When the letters from one grid are
placed in the blank squares of the other
grid, the following message is revealed:

T	O	M	I	H	A	V	E	T	H	E	L	A	S	T
O	F	T	H	E	D	O	G	S	W	E	C	A	N	S
H	I	P	T	H	E	M	O	U	T	O	F	T	H	E
C	I	T	Y	T	O	N	I	G	H	T	A	N	D	S
T	A	R	T	S	E	L	L	I	N	G	T	H	E	M
T	O	M	O	R	R	O	W	K	E	E	P	T	H	I
S	M	E	S	S	A	G	E	S	E	C	R	E	T	I
W	A	N	T	T	H	I	S	D	E	A	L	T	O	B
E	O	U	R	S	A	L	O	N	E	S	H	A	R	I

Page 139:

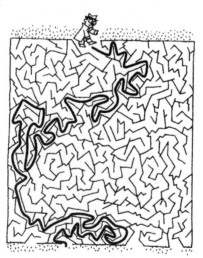

Page 141:

Key D: When viewed from the side, the
teeth on the keys show the number of
the warehouse it opens.

Page 143:

Page 145:

Page 147:

DETECTIVE DAVE,
    AS SOON AS YOU LEFT I
REMEMBERED THAT MISS VAN
ASTERSLOAN WAS GOING TO TAKE
PIERRE INTO THE PET SALON FOR A
SHAMPOO AND HAIRCUT. I AM SORRY
TO HAVE BOTHERED YOU.
    MARTHA

1. eye (not a part of the foot)
2. saw (the other items are used for cleaning)
3. Pete (does not rhyme with the other names)
4. and (the other words can be spelled with the letters A, R, T, S)
5. now (refers to the present, not the past)
6. half (represents a fraction of something, not a whole)
7. A (the other letters are lowercased)
8. knew (the others represent physical action that you can see)
9. hare (not used for transportation)
10. cut (the other words refer to bringing something together)

Say the answers aloud and they read:
I SAW PETE AND NOW HAVE A NEW HAIRCUT.

The two complete letters should say:

DETECTIVE DAVE,
YOU ARE IN DANGER OF MISSING A BIG OPPORTUNITY. IT WOULD BE A CRIME IF YOU MISSED OUR ANNUAL USED UNDERWEAR AND HANDKERCHIEF SALE, NOW THROUGH SATURDAY AT BARNEY'S BARGAIN SHOP.

Detective Dave,
You are just the person I need. Come as soon as you can to 1031 Steep Hill Road. Don't delay. Your help is wanted desperately. I'll be looking for you.

Page 157:

> The dials can be rotated to spell out the
> word *HARE*.

Page 159:

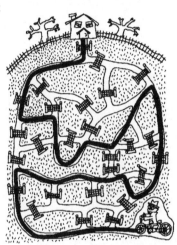

Page 161:

> HA! YOU ARE **I**RAPPED
> IN **H**ERE FOR**E**VER.
> T**R**YING TO **E**SCAPE **I**S
> US**E**LESS. THESE B**A**RS
> ARE UNBREA**K**ABL**E**.
> **Y**OU S**H**OULD G**I**VE
> UP HOPE IMME**D**IATELY.
> **D**ON'T **E**VEN THI**N**K OF
> LEAV**I**NG; TH**I**S C**A**GE
> IS NOW **Y**OUR HOME!

The missing letters from the note spell
out the clue: THERE IS A KEY HIDDEN
IN HAY.

When the books are put in numerical order, the letters on their spines spell out this message:

Page 165:

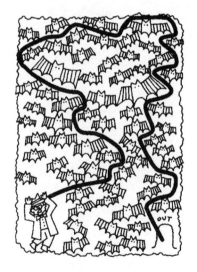

Page 167:

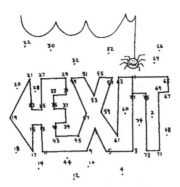

Page 169:

> The keys numbered 9, 3, and 14 add up
> to 26, which is the number above the
> third door.

Page 171:

> The letters on the path spell out the
> message:
>
> IF YOU THINK THIS PUZZLE WAS HARD
> TO SOLVE, JUST WAIT.

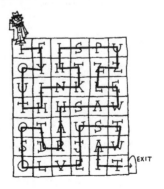

The safe bridge is #5:

Bridges #2 and #4 can be eliminated because they are next to bridge #3, which is made up of an even number of boards (clue #1).

Bridge #3 can be eliminated because it is not built of more boards than either of its neighboring bridges (clue #2).

The safe bridge is between two other bridges (clue #2), which eliminates bridges #1 and #7.

Finally, bridge #6 can be eliminated because it is the only bridge built with five boards (clue #3).

The remaining bridge is #5.

The answers to the alligator's riddle are as follows:
bee (B)
eye (I)
tea (T)
and the letter "E"
Together they spell out the final answer:
BITE

The Electric Door Opener is not plugged in!

Reading downward, the remaining letters spell out:

A SPELL HAS JUST BEEN CAST ON YOU

Page 181:

A frog!

Page 183:

The letters on the scroll are in proper order, with the triangles separating each word. By rotating the letters, the message reads:

Page 185:

Key #5 has no matching twin.

Viewed from the side, the upper half of
the bottle markings read:

> BUG BLOOD
> BEE EYES
> SQUID INK
> BRAIN POWDER
> FLEAS
> FLY DUST

Page 193:

R A T T L E S N A K E

R E T T L A S N E K A

R E T T A L S N E K A

R E D D A L S N E K A

R E D D A L N E K S

R E D D A L P E T S

S T E P L A D D E R

Page 195:

The second page of the letter should read:

I HAVE A BRAND NEW FUN HOUSE RIDE AT MY THEME PARK, BUT I DO NOT WANT IT TO BE TOO HAIR-RAISING FOR LITTLE KIDS. I KNOW YOU ARE THE RIGHT ONE TO TEST IT OUT FOR ME.

Page 197:

The coded message reads:

THANK YOU FOR ALL OF YOUR HELP. AS A TOKEN OF MY APPRECIATION, HERE IS A FREE PASS YOU CAN USE TO VISIT MY FUN HOUSE RIDE AT ANY TIME.

FRANK N. STINE

Page 203:

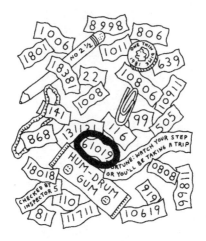

Page 205:

The labels read:
FRANCE (FR + ants)
CUBA (cube + A)
POLAND (pole + and)
TURKEY
JAPAN (JA + pan)
HAITI (hay + T)
NEW ZEALAND (news + eel + and)
CANADA (can + ADA)

Page 207:

Page 209:

> The letters on license plate SLTEA can
> be rearranged to spell:
>   LEAST
>   SLATE
>   STALE
>   STEAL
>   TALES
> (and TEALS, meaning a type of duck, or
> shades of greenish blue)

Page 211:

Page 213:

> The brochures are arranged alphabetically
> by city. The brochure for Garden Grove
> is out of order.

Page 215:

Page 217:

Balloon #3 is identical to the one on the sign.

Page 219:

Page 221:

> Turn the page sideways. The buildings,
> hills, and roads form a message
> pointing to the "LANDING FIELD."

Page 223:

> The computer substituted 1 for A, 2 for
> B, etc. and A for 1, B for 2, etc. This is
> the decoded schedule:
>
> | DESTINATION | BUS NUMBER |
> | --- | --- |
> | SPRINGFIELD | 12 |
> | BLUE VALLEY | 64 |
> | TEENY TOWN | 48 |
> | BLABBERBURG | 37 |
> | RIVER CITY | 36 |
> | MEGAVILLE | 51 |
>
> Bus #36 is headed to River City.

Page 225:

> The least expensive way to River City is
> by donkey cart.
>
> Donkey cart = $2.50 x 5 hours =
> $12.50
>
> Vivian's Vans = $26.00 x 1/2 hour =
> $13.00
>
> Cab = ($.50 x 20 miles) + ($2.00 x 2
> people) = $14.00
>
> LuAnn's Limos = $.75 x 20 miles =
> $15.00
>
> WE-HAUL = $18.00
>
> Airplane = $10.00 x 2 people = $20.00

Page 227:

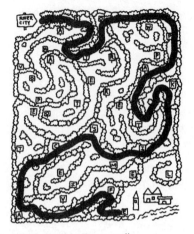

The letters on the signs spell:
STOP AT KIM'S CAFE

Page 229:

DEAR MOTHER

MY TRIP HAS
NOT GONE AS
PLANNED. I THINK
I AM BEING
FOLLOWED BY TWO
STRANGERS. I
HOPE TO LOSE
THEM ON THE
FERRY RIDE I AM
TAKING IN A FEW
MINUTES.

Page 231:

Boats B and D are tied to each other.
Boat C is tied to the buoy. Boat A must
be the boat tied to the ferry, even
though all of its rope is not visible.

Page 233:

> The ferry captain's uncle must own the first shop. The other two shops are owned by women.

Page 235:

> The three items, one from each row, that total $18 are:
>
> • the $7 piggy bank
>
> • the $5 salt and pepper shakers
>
> • the $6 T-shirt
>
> They all say PIG CITY.

Page 237:

Page 239:

> Miss Chiff tried to fool Detective Dave by turning the sign upside down: It reads:
>
> SUNNYSIDE
> INN
> ONE
> MILE

Page 241:

BELLHOP~ DON'T FORGET TO
PICK UP THE SUITCASES
OUTSIDE OF ROOM
8. THEY BELONG TO MISS
SMITH. THERE SHOULD BE
2. THEY WON'T BE HEAVY. THEN
BRING A CUP OF TEA TO MISS
CHIFF WHO IS IN ROOM
20. THANKS.

Page 243:

THE WOMAN WE WERE FOLLOWING
WAS NOT MISS TERRY CHIFF. IT WAS
HER IDENTICAL TWIN SISTER, MISS
SHERRI CHIFF.

Page 245:

The circled words spell the message:

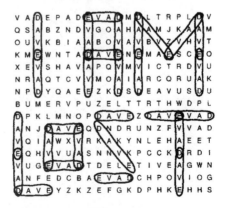

**If you like this book,
look for these other mighty big,
mighty fun
Mighty Big Books**